LIVING WITH PURPOSE

LIVING WITH PURPOSE

TRISTAN EVERGREEN

CONTENTS

CHAPTER 1

Chapter 1: Introduction

For most of human history, our species has grappled with dilemmas that pose profound questions rooted in ancient myths and folklore: Why am I here? What is my place in the world, and what kind of value can I contribute? These questions bridge the chasm between what exists and what is possible, forming the foundation of our quest for meaning. Could solving these ancient dilemmas be our birthright? Could regaining this ancient perspective usher in a new era of empowerment for humanity, offering solutions to many of the world's modern problems?

Embarking on this journey, we discover the ultimate source of purpose and meaning. Living with a strong sense of purpose is a unique and inspirational gift, unfolding our greatest expressions of joy, fulfillment, and happiness. Our journey epitomizes a relentless pursuit of meaning, rediscovering an empowering way of thought that aligns us with the cosmos, our unique gifts of creation, and the realization of our highest potential.

If asked, could you clearly articulate your mission in life? Defining your purpose provides direction and meaning to your daily existence. Consequently, a profound sense of fulfillment and joy often benefits those who have clearly identified their purpose. Are you one of these people? The source of potential purpose is the driving motivation behind our ability to evolve, contribute, and create solutions to the world's most pressing problems. This capacity originates from an extraordinary ability to harness the power of thoughts, emotions, and creative impulses locked deep within us. However, this universal energy often lies dormant, overshadowed by routine obligations and societal expectations.

Understanding the Importance of Living with Purpose

Her story astounded me. When you think of CIA operatives, you probably envision characters like Jason Bourne—skilled in bloodshed, extreme acrobatics, and navigating perilous situations. The lovely woman across the aisle shared some similarities, though in a different field. She never once spoke of how she gave Shallon away because her job wouldn't allow the freedom of raising a child. Never once did she change her tone when she spoke of these things, or anything else, for that matter. At first, I wondered if there was simply nothing deeper to find in her actions. But when she asked me how I was doing, I started to ponder purpose, to question myself and the things I value most. Our purpose is guided by our values, revealed through our decisions. Her decisions, and their drastic consequences, painted her as an altruistic and fiercely dedicated woman, willing to do anything to serve people she would never meet or save countries she would never see.

On a cross-country flight, I found myself seated next to an older woman with striking blue eyes and a warm smile. Before we even reached our cruising altitude, a friendly conversation began. I quickly learned that this beautiful lady had lived an amazing and dangerous life thirty-plus years ago. Usually, the most incredible encounters while traveling happen within the pages of a book. I count myself incredibly lucky that day, the day I flew with a retired CIA agent hidden beneath a lovely demeanor. That day marked a significant turning point for me; for the first time, I truly understood what it meant to live with purpose.

Identifying Your Why

Identifying the reasons for your existence is an important yet complex step in the purpose-exploration process. Answering the question "Why do I exist?" allows us to decide for ourselves what our lives mean and what we truly value and believe, rather than letting others decide for us. By questioning the sources of our values and beliefs—our families, schools, or culture—we can reject those sources and redevelop our values and beliefs in a form that is uniquely our own.

Often, however, purpose is not self-identified; we seek it out in a combination of messages from our families, schools, and culture, and sometimes we don't receive positive messages at all. Discovering your purpose is a deeply personal experience, and there may be no one-size-fits-all solution. After all, it is this purpose that provides our lives with deep meaning, passion, and fulfillment, fueling the pursuit of our dreams.

Start your purpose journey by asking yourself one simple question: "Why do I exist?" Although the question is simple, the answers can be complex. Dr. Michael Steger suggests that there may be multiple answers to the question of existence—for example, "I exist to promote the general well-being of everyone I encounter," and "to be a loving mother." These answers represent what matters most in a person's life and can change and evolve over time.

Chapter 2: Discovering Your Passions

What Are Our Passions?

Over the years, I have come to believe that identifying my own passions has been easier than discovering the passions of others. In conventional terms, our passions might be found in the volunteer endeavors, special causes, hobbies, or interests that excite us. They might be found in the learning and challenges we crave, or in the playful and creative activities, travel, or adventures that lead us to our greatest moments of engagement and fulfillment. At the heart of discovering our personal passions is something yet more complex: we must get to know ourselves and understand the roles we play in the greater scheme of things—in the present, as the resolution of the past, and as part of the continuum of a potential future.

Entrepreneurs often start new business ventures because they find a niche in a particular market and create a product or service to fill it. Similarly, nonprofit organizations emerge to address gaps where the market or government cannot meet certain needs. Often, people start organizations around issues for which they have a personal passion. Passion for evidence-based policymaking, coaching kids, and working with other women are among the stories our panelists shared at a staff retreat in early 2012. This week's blog is about discovering our passions and Dr. Tom Suddendorf's theory of how humans are unique and how we celebrate our uniqueness by supporting and pursuing the passions of others.

Exploring Different Areas of Interest

We have to explore. The answers to finding your passion live everywhere we look and within everything we experience. Specific actions, such as reading or traveling, can help you explore different things that you might love. Moreover, we must be mindful of everything we do. Take time to listen to what you say yes to and what you say no to. What inspires you? What drives you? What do you admire? What angers you? Everything we encounter in life holds the potential to help us explore and realize our passions. This is not something you can sit back and hope to accomplish one day. It's also not about changing careers or making a huge move. You can start now and let daily musings guide you.

It sounds simple enough, but it's not as easy as it seems. Nowadays, teenagers are put on paths and take crowded roads to attend classes throughout grade school. Then decisions must be made about a degree, or job versus two-year college. There are so many choices that it can be difficult to decide if you're doing what you love, or if you're just being the best possible version of what you're not really sure about. We live in a day and age where many of us live for vacations or can't wait until Friday, even when it seems like we don't enjoy most of the days leading up to that vacation or Friday. Is it always about taking the good with the bad? What if there is more good than bad? What if we can begin enjoying ten great days for every one bad? How do we find what it is we would want to fill our days with?

Reflecting on Your Strengths and Values

Understanding your values helps us better understand ourselves and can resolve conflicts in many situations. Senior citizens often talk about values being the fundamentals that shape choices. The most frequent piece of advice was, "When it comes to your values, don't compromise." This is especially important as there may be times in life when important values are being challenged—like not withholding information and not gossiping. Goals should align with the most important values in our lives. If not, the goals and values will interrelate in some negative way. Values are crucial in your purposeful approach to life. Values you constantly use are your core values as they shape your life—like your lifestyle. They are the fundamentals or foundations. You probably learned these values by observing other people, so they are likely general beliefs shared by those in your main network who influenced you as you grew up. Values also get updated and internalized. Often these valuable life-enforced principles are acquired from a loved parent, Big Brother or Sister, a teacher, or a coach who spends lots of time with you to help you reach your full potential. You internalize those values and take them for granted as part of your personal beliefs. Personal achievements result when your goals match your personal values and they are consistent. What we stand for and believe in makes us better individuals.

An important part of finding your why is determining what makes you unique. What sets you apart from everyone else? What are your strengths? What are your talents? What are the things you are passionate about and what are your values? Many people don't want to talk about their strengths or talents because they are too modest or it feels like bragging. But the truth is, what makes you different makes you compelling and interesting. Many opportunities you have in life will come from someone making a personal connection with you, and that's impossible if they don't know what your strengths are. Celebrating your talents can also serve as a powerful role model for others. Understand how your talents can add value to society and help achieve your purpose in life, and by sharing that message, you may be able to encourage others to do the same.

Experimenting with New Activities

One of these experiments might feel like it's what you've been missing all your life. That's when you find your passion. It's that thing you could do for free for the rest of your life and be happy doing. It's something you never get tired of. It's that creative energy that keeps you up at night. Do you know your passion? If not, don't worry—it's a process, and it will come to you eventually. On the other hand, if you already know what you're passionate about, that too is just the beginning. You know the three basic steps to get something done: find a mentor, be the beginner, and cross the "fire swamp". With a passion or purpose in your life, it's time to venture out into the world and see what difference you can make.

One way to chase your dreams is by trying new activities. How do you know you're not great at playing the piano if you've never tried? Or that you weren't born to be the best salesperson for your company? We often surprise ourselves by doing activities we never thought we could do. The only way to find out if we're good at something or love doing it is by trying. It's through this experimenting that we learn about life and ourselves. Some things will feel like second nature, while others will feel like a battle. This is a sign of what path you should be on. Accurately recognizing those signs can lead you to make better decisions and use your life to chase your dreams.

Chapter 3: Setting Meaningful Goals

Setting meaningful goals is essential for living a purposeful and fulfilling life. By studying our "peak experiences," we identify activities that bring us the most joy and satisfaction. These moments, both at work and outside of it, deeply involve us and evoke extremely positive emotions. To continuously improve, we carve time on our calendars for deliberate practice—activities that challenge us to go beyond our current skill level. We use doable activities to gain confidence and make progress toward meaningful endeavors. For instance, if writing a book and producing a podcast are meaningful but daunting tasks, we might start with writing as our doable activity to make progress without feeling overwhelmed by the larger task. Finally, we commit to improving everyone's well-being: ours, our family's, our friends', and so on.

"Prioritize activities that are difficult but not urgent or overly time-consuming." Meaningful activities tend to be challenging because they require us to display our best selves or fulfill something that deeply resonates with us. These meaningful goals are often not immediately doable; they are aspirations to pursue, not just tasks to check off our weekly to-do lists. For example, stepping out of our comfort zone at work to suggest a new way to profile users might require months or even years of extra effort. As the goal is meaningful, we should start it and always know the next smallest step toward its achievement.

Defining Your Long-Term Vision

When we decide to change the game, to recover our inner thirst to truly flourish and meet life's demands, everything changes. With the mass amount of negativity and countless distractions, especially from new technologies, basic life decisions can become hazy. But within every heart lies the compass that can guide us to joyful and purposeful life satisfaction. You just need to identify what you want to happen. This will be your long-term vision. It's been called your right-livelihood, finding your why, your destiny, your true passion, and more. Whatever name you give it, one thing is true: a clear, internal vision can be the compass that guides both short and long-term goals.

Committing to creating and living a life based on what matters most to you can change the entire landscape of your existence. Within the circle of life lie the inner desires and dreams within your heart. When these internal plants are unsupported or not watered, they become weak and start to wilt. Instead of thriving and feeling purposeful, life can turn into a mechanical existence filled with unfulfilling daily habits, spurred by jobs, relationships, and activities that compromise your unique imaginations in an attempt to please others. There's purpose behind the day-to-day habits we've adopted. We all gain something from every relationship, choice, and general activity.

Breaking Down Goals into Manageable Steps

Let's break everything down into manageable chunks. You've identified your dream and the smaller goals that will help you get there. Now, sit down and identify the steps to those goals. Let's take an example that many people can relate to: you've dreamed of visiting all seven continents. To do this, you need money. One of your goals is to save money for this adventure. A step towards saving money is figuring out how much you need to save. Another step could be researching the cost of traveling to each continent. With a realistic cost in mind, you can develop a plan to start saving. Each step may require additional research or a list of steps to refine and break things down into bite-size pieces. Take the time to work through what you need to do to achieve those goals, and before you know it, you'll be climbing your mountain.

"The journey of a thousand miles begins with one step." - Lao Tzu. We've all heard this cliche, but its truth often gets lost in its simplicity. We may have big goals and dreams, but we cannot simply achieve them in one giant leap. We need to establish smaller steps to make our end goal a reality. Let's use mountain climbing as an example. If you're standing at the base of a mountain and try to leap to the top in one jump, you'll likely fall back down. However, if you take the time to carefully step from one stone to the next, no matter how high the mountain appears, you will slowly make your way to the top. Stepping stones. They take something huge and intimidating and break it down into manageable bits. It seems simple, and in a way, it is, but it takes focus and determination to actually do it.

Creating a Timeline for Achievement

"Persons who entirely escape the risk of defeat also escape the possibility of experiencing the exhilaration of having conquered." - Andrew Carnegie. Setting a deadline helps us be more efficient with time. Without deadlines, we have a general idea of when we want to complete a goal, but we also know we have time to spare. This can lead to training less, taking more off days than necessary, and never really stretching beyond our comfort zone. Organizer guru Anthony Robbins talks about setting a "compelling future." He states: "In fact, if we think that completing a project in three weeks would be very compelling, the project becomes compelling." Deadlines represent a finish line. When we shorten the timeline, we move the finish line closer to the present, making things more urgent. Once urgency is present, you are more ready to tackle the subject, becoming more focused and efficient.

Continuing with Brian's book "Goal Setting," this chapter will be Chapter Five, where he discusses setting timelines for goal setting. We all know how important deadlines are for any goals we want to achieve. In fact, it is widely believed that a goal is simply a dream if there is no deadline. Deadlines are important for several reasons. First, by setting a deadline, you give yourself a target to shoot for. You now have a line in the sand and a date on the calendar to measure success. Without a deadline, you don't know how much time you have to prepare for your outcome. A project that takes a year to complete will look very different from a project that takes twenty years, as a larger time frame allows for more contingency. Many people get by with this ambiguity, but not you. An ordinary life simply will not do.

Chapter 4: Overcoming Obstacles and Challenges

As we chase our dreams, we encounter various challenges, both usual and personal. These challenges are natural and serve a deliberate purpose in our journey. With self-discipline, we can overcome these obstacles. Here are some tips to help you tackle both types of challenges. Personal challenges range from making excuses for failure to emotional entanglement and patterns of negative thoughts. A good way to overcome most challenges is to remind yourself of your purpose. When negative emotions arise, and a sense of failure threatens to block your progress, using positive reinforcement and recalling your purpose will help you get back on track. Developing a good self-image and setting meaningful goals can also be effective. Knowing what you want and deserve, and prioritizing yourself respectfully, will keep you focused on your dreams. Going negative because of initial failures will only hinder your progress and may ultimately erase your dreams.

Developing Resilience and Perseverance

Developing resilience and perseverance involves finding the strength to maintain realistic focus and a constructive attitude in the face of adversity. It's not just about resisting but about using the strength gained from suffering to move forward. To develop resilience, talk to other people, seek professional help, take care of your health (mental and physical), and recognize your faults and difficulties. Finding strategies to improve these areas is a great way to start. Recent research in psychology shows that resilience and perseverance are strongly related to other psychological variables such as mental health, depression, anxiety, and self-esteem. Learning to overcome bad moments with dedication and focus will turn into personal strength over time.

The most challenging and important skills to develop are resilience and perseverance. These are transversal skills that will take you to any dream or goal. Resilience refers to the psychological ability to successfully face adversities, overcome challenges of trauma, stress, tragedy, threats, or significant sources of danger. Building resilience is about adapting positively to adverse situations, rather than destructively. Perseverance means continuing with consistency and dedication towards a goal. Studies show that these two abilities are essential for advancing towards professional, personal, and academic goals. Developing both skills implies other individual abilities or attitudes will also be developed. Perseverance involves showing resilience by facing fears, adversities, and uncertainties, accepting that it will take time and work, and that failure may come. However, resilience alone doesn't explain consistency towards a specific goal.

Seeking Support from Others

An educational community makes the entire process of learning during the adventure easier. It makes experiences more real, embeds understanding deeper in our brains, and keeps us accountable to our goals once the novelty has waned. You can view others' enthusiasm for something and feed off that energy. Living with purpose in our own lives can inspire others to do the same. Our stories can evoke admiration and maybe cause a little bit of jealousy at first, but eventually inspire friends to embrace adventure and seek unconventional paths. Every adventure, to someone else, may be seen as an unconventional life.

Seek out and find a supportive community of like-minded, goal-driven individuals on your journey to living with purpose. A solid local community of friends and mentors is key to keeping grounded. Genuine conversations and values are more important than any material possessions. A community of individuals sharing similar passions will enrich your experiences. Do you want to become a better photographer? Join a photography club, attend critique groups, and find mentors. Doing so will catapult your craft.

Embracing Failure as a Learning Opportunity

As the world-famous innovator Thomas Edison said, "I have not failed. I've just found 10,000 ways that won't work." Believing that every unsuccessful attempt brings you one step closer to success is crucial. Making mistakes, failing, and never giving up on your commitment to what you believe in helps elevate you to the next level. You always have to keep evolving, adapting, learning, and being aware of your aspirations. Recognize there's room at the top for everyone, but not everyone is meant to be an innovator. Not everyone is prepared to make sacrifices, and not everyone can put plans ahead of passions, even though you have the potential to be.

Whether you are just starting your journey or are a seasoned professional, you will always be challenged in your field because the rules are always changing. New technologies or best practices are constantly being discovered, and it can be emotionally and mentally challenging. Embrace failure and see change as a good thing. Understand that failure is a necessary step on the path to success. To stay successful in your career, you may need to constantly change and evolve, and you will be met with failure possibly on a daily basis. The key to success is the drive, ambition, and passion to make a difference. Despite the great results, leaders who can withstand failure and understand that failing is part of the journey recognize that failure is significant progress towards future successes.

Chapter 5: Taking Action and Making Changes

Life happens, right? Ultimately, we need to adjust and find something that reinvigorates and re-inspires us, giving us a renewed purpose. Often, we're not adaptive to changes in our circumstances, or we fall into negative habits that hinder our progress. While psychology and self-help offer many good ideas and exercises, it's common to know them but not practice them.

The key is to create an environment that supports your goals and surrounds you with people who inspire you and share your drive. Breaking out of negative cycles requires action and decision-making. Many people hear motivational messages but don't take the necessary action steps to make a change. It's a state of adaptation that we need to overcome.

Implementing Strategies for Personal Growth

A remarkable journey is always evolving and growing, creating a genuine sense of passion for your purpose. Use your unique talents to craft the purpose you seek in life. Opportunity is accessible at every turn, and this week, I challenge you to step around it and chase your dreams.

- **Set Goals:** They can be small, big, or anywhere in between. Clear-cut goals help measure your progress and guide you towards your purpose.
- **Create a Schedule:** Day in and day out, your life is filled with tasks, appointments, meals, work, etc. A schedule can drastically improve your productivity.
- **Learn from Each Situation:** It's important to withstand the journey, always leaving room for growth. Living in the present helps you accomplish your goals and ultimately be at peace with yourself.
- **Reflect on Your Accomplishments:** Reflecting on what you've achieved is an effective way to ensure you're on your way to pursuing your purpose.
- **Implement a Work-Life Balance:** Ensure your work allows space for life experiences. Gaining experiences and independence outside of work is healthy.

Personal growth is a continuous journey, and it's never too late to start. By taking actionable steps every day to better yourself, you will in turn better the world around you. Here are a few personal growth strategies that have helped me on my purposeful journey.

Making Decisions Aligned with Your Purpose

If you are still unsure of your purpose or are in the midst of confusion, here are a few tips to help you find your why:

- **Let Go of Fearful Mindsets:** Release unproductive mindsets that prevent you from accepting and loving yourself deeply.
- **Reflect on Recurring Thoughts:** Ask yourself what drives you to take action and identify recurring desires or thoughts you've had since you were young.

- **Focus on Joyful Moments:** Reflect on times filled with joy and happiness. These moments often align with your purpose.

Once you discover your why, it becomes the center of your decisions. Your why is the essence of who you are—it's your deepest desire, belief, and value. With a clear why, you make decisions that align with your purpose, leading to extraordinary outcomes. You will find that decisions become easier when they are in harmony with who you are. You'll live each day with purpose and excitement, knowing you are moving closer to your dreams.

Embracing Change and Adaptability

Learning to adapt when things don't go as planned is crucial. Your current self wouldn't exist without the series of events that have changed you throughout your life. When change seems daunting or out of your control, remember that these experiences have shaped who you are today. Embrace the fear of the unknown and make an effort to live a life full of love and passion. Adaptability empowers you to chase your dreams without hesitation, freeing you from the comfort zone and fueling your actions.

We often let fear of the unknown paralyze us from beginning anything meaningful. The fear of failing, judgment from others, or simply not knowing how to proceed can stop us in our tracks. The truth is, the unknown is scary but also exhilarating, full of endless possibilities. Overcome these fears and take the first step towards change—your future self will thank you. When faced with change that has a lasting effect on your life, trust yourself to make the right decision. It's a strange feeling to rely on intuition, but answers are usually more rooted in your heart than your head. Trust your instincts and believe in your capabilities and worth.

Chapter 6: Finding Balance and Prioritizing Self-C

In the pursuit of our dreams, finding balance and prioritizing self-care is crucial. It's easy to get caught up in the hustle and bustle of daily life, but without balance and self-care, we risk burnout and decreased productivity. This chapter will explore how to manage your time and energy effectively, nurture your physical and mental well-being, and cultivate healthy relationships.

Managing Time and Energy Effectively

Managing time and energy effectively is essential for achieving your goals without feeling overwhelmed. Here are some strategies to help you make the most of your time and energy:

- **Prioritize Tasks:** Identify what tasks are most important and tackle them first. Use tools like to-do lists or digital planners to keep track of your priorities.
- **Set Boundaries:** Learn to say no to activities that do not align with your goals or drain your energy. It's okay to protect your time.

- **Break Down Tasks:** Divide larger tasks into smaller, manageable steps. This makes them less daunting and helps maintain your momentum.
- **Schedule Downtime:** Just as you schedule work tasks, schedule time for rest and relaxation. This helps recharge your energy and prevent burnout.
- **Practice Time Blocking:** Allocate specific blocks of time for different activities throughout your day. This helps you stay focused and ensures you dedicate time to various aspects of your life.
- **Limit Distractions:** Identify what distracts you and find ways to minimize these interruptions. This might mean turning off notifications, setting a specific work area, or using focus-enhancing techniques like the Pomodoro method.

Nurturing Your Physical and Mental Well-being

Your physical and mental health are vital components of self-care and balance. Here are ways to nurture both:

- **Regular Exercise:** Incorporate physical activity into your daily routine. Exercise not only boosts your physical health but also improves mental clarity and mood.
- **Healthy Eating:** Fuel your body with nutritious foods that provide sustained energy. Pay attention to what you eat and how it makes you feel.
- **Adequate Sleep:** Ensure you get enough sleep each night. Quality sleep is crucial for overall health and well-being, affecting everything from cognitive function to emotional stability.

- **Mindfulness and Meditation:** Practice mindfulness or meditation to reduce stress and increase mental clarity. These practices help you stay grounded and focused.
- **Seek Professional Help:** If you're struggling with mental health issues, don't hesitate to seek professional support. Therapy and counseling can provide valuable tools and insights for managing your well-being.
- **Self-Reflection:** Take time to reflect on your thoughts and feelings. Journaling or engaging in introspective practices can help you understand yourself better and make informed decisions about your well-being.

Cultivating Healthy Relationships

Building and maintaining healthy relationships is a key aspect of self-care and balance. Here are some tips for cultivating strong connections with others:

- **Effective Communication:** Practice clear and open communication with the people in your life. Express your needs and listen actively to others.
- **Set Boundaries:** Establish boundaries that protect your well-being and ensure relationships are mutually respectful.
- **Quality Time:** Spend quality time with loved ones. Engage in activities that strengthen your bond and create lasting memories.
- **Surround Yourself with Positivity:** Choose to spend time with people who uplift and support you. Positive relationships can enhance your emotional well-being and provide a strong support system.

- **Resolve Conflicts:** Address conflicts directly and construc-tively. Work towards understanding and finding solutions rather than letting issues fester.
- **Show Appreciation:** Regularly express gratitude and appre-ciation for the people in your life. Acknowledging their pos-itive impact strengthens your relationships and fosters a supportive network.

By managing your time and energy effectively, nurturing your physical and mental well-being, and cultivating healthy relation-ships, you can achieve a balanced and fulfilling life. Prioritizing self-care allows you to chase your dreams with renewed energy and a clear mind.

Chapter 7: Celebrating Milestones and Successes

Celebrating milestones and successes is essential for maintaining motivation and recognizing the progress you've made on your journey. Acknowledging achievements, rewarding yourself, and sharing your journey with others can create a positive feedback loop that fuels further success.

Recognizing and Acknowledging Achievements

Recognizing and acknowledging achievements is crucial for sustaining motivation and building self-confidence. Here are some ways to do this effectively:

- **Keep a Journal:** Document your accomplishments, big and small. Reflecting on your achievements helps you see the progress you've made and boosts your morale.
- **Set Milestones:** Break down your goals into smaller milestones. Celebrate reaching each milestone as it brings you closer to your larger goal.
- **Reflect Regularly:** Take time to reflect on what you've accomplished. Acknowledge the hard work and dedication it took to get there.

- **Share Your Successes:** Share your achievements with friends, family, or a supportive community. Their encouragement can reinforce your sense of accomplishment.
- **Create a Visual Reminder:** Display your achievements in a place where you can see them daily. This could be a vision board, a wall of photos, or a digital scrapbook.

Rewarding Yourself for Progress

Rewarding yourself for progress, no matter how small, can keep you motivated and make the journey enjoyable. Here are some ideas for rewarding yourself:

- **Celebrate Small Wins:** Treat yourself when you reach small milestones. It could be something simple like enjoying a favorite treat or taking a relaxing day off.
- **Plan Bigger Rewards:** For significant achievements, plan more substantial rewards. This could be a weekend getaway, a special dinner, or purchasing something you've wanted for a while.
- **Incorporate Fun:** Integrate fun activities into your routine as rewards for meeting your goals. This keeps the process enjoyable and gives you something to look forward to.
- **Reward Effort, Not Just Results:** Recognize the effort you put into working toward your goals, even if the results aren't immediate. Consistent effort deserves to be celebrated.
- **Celebrate with Loved Ones:** Share your rewards with friends or family. Celebrating together can strengthen your relationships and make the achievements feel even more special.

Sharing Your Journey with Others

Sharing your journey with others can provide inspiration, support, and accountability. Here are some ways to do this:

- **Join a Community:** Become part of a group or community that shares similar goals. This can provide a support network and a platform to share your progress.
- **Mentor Others:** Share your experiences and insights with those who are on a similar path. Mentoring can be incredibly fulfilling and reinforces your own learning.
- **Use Social Media:** Share your milestones and successes on social media. This can inspire others and create a sense of accountability.
- **Write About It:** Start a blog, journal, or write articles about your journey. Documenting your experiences can help you reflect and share valuable lessons with a wider audience.
- **Celebrate Together:** Organize gatherings or events to celebrate milestones with friends, family, or colleagues. Sharing your journey with others can make the achievements feel even more rewarding.

Chapter 8: Sustaining Motivation and Momentum

Sustaining motivation requires the repetitive act of revisiting the WHYs of life. Knowing what we are all about and pursuing it relentlessly has been documented time and again as essential for success. Georges St-Pierre, winner of numerous world titles in multiple weight classes and one of the greatest fighters in mixed martial arts (MMA) history, wrote in his autobiography, "The Way of the Fight," about the value of setting high, yet realistic, goals and working harder than anyone else leading up to an event. As you work toward any goal, remember these lessons from Georges St-Pierre and others: sustain effort and touch on potential below the surface.

Regarding motivation, people often mention confidence, fear, and desire. Confidence, or belief in oneself, acts as the glue that holds fears and desires together. It is the belief that you have the ability to act in a given pursuit.

In the quest for success, the ability to persist and recover after failure is imperative to translating your dreams into reality. Whether it's living with purpose, scaling up your legacy, or any other mission, motivation, direction, and alignment with the task are necessary.

Given the constant and accelerating changes in the world, our purpose—and therefore our motivation and direction—will also evolve. The key to self-actualization is engaging in activities of sustained challenge, basing our actions on enduring principles that do not change.

Cultivating a Growth Mindset

Many people underestimate the power that comes from nurturing the right mindset. People look at success and readily conclude that some are just lucky, favored by fate, or simply out to get them. The good news is that you can cultivate a growth mindset! It is not something you are born with but a habit and choice you make daily.

The most powerful lesson from Carol Dweck's research on mindset is that if you are truly dedicated to personal growth, you don't have to change who you are. You only need to approach life from a different philosophical angle. Researchers have found that people with a growth mindset are not overly concerned with proving themselves to others. They are more focused on improving themselves. If you find yourself always trying to prove something to someone, it's possible you are engaging a fixed mindset. But don't worry—you can change that starting now!

We often have a love-love relationship with our comfort zone. We dwell there to celebrate achievements, seek it when licking the invisible wounds of a failed plan, and constantly seek items to add to our comfort zone inventory. While it is great to stay in your comfort zone, you may soon start feeling complacent, doubting if you can or should try something new, or even wondering if you deserve better than what you have now. This is the point where I encourage you to lean into discomfort. Identify at least one thing today that makes you uncomfortable and persistently do it. Growth lies on the opposite side of your comfort zone. For all you know, that one thing could be the game changer you have been yearning for!

Finding Inspiration in Everyday Life

Eight months ago, for the holidays, my girlfriend gave me a gift I was completely unfamiliar with—a sketchbook. Though I initially only wrote "thanks" on its first page, deep down, I decided to use it and fill it entirely. Maintaining this commitment was easy as it was a private project, and making a mission statement over a blank notebook felt unnecessary. However, as I continued to fill its pages, my perspective began to shift. I discovered that inspiration can only find those who actively seek it. It doesn't just come to you; scrolling through endless memes won't make it appear.

The ideas of creativity and inspiration had been foreign to me for as long as I could remember. My strategy in terms of work, personal projects, and the like had always been to put in the necessary hours. I worked my way to accomplishments and took pride in that. But eventually, the cycle of grinding away just to achieve a new goal, only to set new ones and immediately delve into them, felt pointless. The more I thought about being creative or inspired, the more I realized that inspiration needed to be actively sought.

Reviewing and Adjusting Goals as Needed

The impact of temporary highs was fleeting. I would feel their effects repeatedly but ultimately found it a lousy way to live. In my late 40s, I decided to think about what I truly wanted. What kind of experiences did I want to have, and where? How much money would I need to make it happen? The biggest decision I made was to become the best person I could be. To do that, I needed to stay sober, keep learning, and be mindful all the time. I set a goal of leaving my fortune to a charitable foundation and formed a plan to accomplish it. From that, I decided to take a real risk with the goal of leaving an important legacy by running for office. Forming a comprehensive plan and working that plan finally provided sustained satisfaction, excitement, and happiness.

The only way to keep growing is by regularly reviewing and adjusting our goals as needed. For most of my life, I set goals to do something or experience something rather than to become something or someone. My adult life often lacked meaning or purpose beyond the momentary high of achievement. The temporary satisfaction would fade, and I would grasp for the next high. I would get excited, but the high was always temporary. I would get busy competing, making more money, moving up the corporate ladder, or feeding one of my addictions. The temporary high would come and go, but nothing changed.

Regularly reviewing and adjusting goals is essential for sustained growth. It allows you to align your actions with your evolving purpose and ensures that your motivation and direction stay relevant. By doing so, you can continue to achieve meaningful and lasting success.

Chapter 9: Creating a Legacy and Making a Differen

Having identified your purpose, why are you living it? Comfort is the primary killer of purpose. People can get on their path or realize the path they should be on, but then they can become comfortable and stop taking action on their purpose or passion. For example, Andrei in Romania is living his dream life, but he could now retire and enjoy a beautiful lifestyle solely focused on himself. Yet, he continues to raise money for charities and orphanages. His passion for education drives him because of the impact, influence, leadership, and connection it provides. For me, it's progression. It could be learning new things, creating something, seeing societal improvement, or just personal progress, but the day I become comfortable is the day I die inside. Assistants who read this article might not care about my message because they're not progressing or improving their style. They might be leading life on default settings.

A big goal like making a difference might make you feel good in the short term, but it's important to have something to aim for that is right for you, something that inspires you personally. So, how do you identify your purpose or that big "why" that makes you get up in the morning? There are many tools to help you identify your purpose or vision. I have friends who used seven different tools to identify their purpose, then took an average. There's the Art of Well-being Journal, which is a bit emotional but helps people uncover what they're passionate about and love. If that's not your type, a simpler approach is using the 'spirit animal' quiz technique. Write down everything you're good at, everything you enjoy, where you see society improving, everything you want to improve in yourself and your society, and then match characteristics of those who inspire you.

Leaving a Positive Impact on Others

Every single person on earth is part of the universal importance of leaving behind a positive impact. Every life action you take or do not take creates endless ripples, emphasizing the personal urgency of doing well and not giving in to neglect or abandonment.

The most significant aspect to consider is not just the effect on individuals, nor the number of people affected, but the center of the ripple—the individual who exercised the actions. Every time you exercise a positive action, you feel a positive release of inner stimuli, generating a ripple of positive actions. In the long-term, these positive ripples produced by others' actions eventually influence you positively. Therefore, every good deed you execute towards others eventually reaches you. This powerful truth is significant in the context of the individual's pursuit of purpose.

Often, we focus on the positive or negative effects we produce on our family and close friends, rationalizing that they are the people permanently part of our lives. However, this rationale dismisses an important reality: the web of human interactions is constantly expanding. Every second, the number of people added to the equation of life grows. Your positive actions affect others who are not part of your immediate reality, just as negative actions do. This is proof that every thought, negative word, or hurtful action causes ripples that expand to the collateral contact area between human beings.

Visualize and internalize the notion that every single human action has a positive or negative effect. In some cases, actions lead to neutral effects. Our society's prosperity results from the actions (good or bad) of countless human beings. Therefore, the hyper-complex web of life that emerges from these interactions is the sum of the positive and negative effects of all human actions.

Giving Back to Your Community

Imagine how different the world would be without jealousy, the urge to climb on top of others to succeed, or the danger of being taken advantage of. Most importantly, people would have a purpose in their lives, exposed to many things without being ostracized. Plus, no one reaching retirement would feel alone or obsolete, as their knowledge, wisdom, and experience would form the foundation for the next generation. They would feel alive. You could be a bridge that supports many travelers to their destination. Without you, they could become wandering souls without purpose. What if they were the person who could find a cure for your beloved sick mother or your dad, who lost his mind due to war remnants? Or what if they were the one who brought peace to the world? As long as you live in it, you have the opportunity to do whatever you want.

Success in many areas of your life often leads to altruism, the act of giving back to the community. This goes deeper than just helping your loved ones; it's about helping anyone and everyone needing guidance, aid, or help. The more people you impact through your achievements, the more successful you become. What if all successful people not only gave back to the community financially but also shared their path, struggles, knowledge, and experience? Most importantly, what if they took the time to give advice and guide the younger generation?

Inspiring and Empowering Others to Find Their Why

Many people inspired and empowered me to make this shift, each with their wisdom and stories of overcoming different issues. While I learn from so many people, I want to mention a few to remind myself and everyone else that we do not have to be alone in our journey to find our why and live a purpose-driven life. Awareness of the inspiration and empowerment you feel can fuel your own awakening or evolution.

The last six months of my life have seen an awakening of sorts—an evolution. I started feeling a need to advocate for living with purpose. I met several people who inspired me through their stories and actions and went through the process of accepting that I could inspire and empower others to find their why. The denial, fear, and anxiety I felt contradicted my why, which is to "Inspire and Empower People to Find their Why and Live a Purpose-Driven Life." Ironically, I advocate manifesting your why on a small scale in your life, such as at work. Yet, I constantly tackled big dreams and goals, as well as the mental hurdles I had to overcome.